Eric Orton

W0472715

The Red Mini

Ferdinand Schöningh 43 501

Contents

Alle Rechte, auch die des auszugsweisen Nachdrucks und der fotomechanischen Wiedergabe, vorbehalten.

© Ferdinand Schöningh, Paderborn. Germany.
Herstellung: Ferdinand Schöningh, Paderborn.
ISBN 3-506-43501-9

A car called Sheila

Do you like the name Sheila? I do! I know three girls called Sheila, and they are all nice. But the Sheila in this true story isn't a girl. She is a car, a new red Mini, registration number 235 GUY. She belongs to Mr. Alan Cooper, 14 Green Lane, Birmingham 3, and he loves her. The Mini Sheila is a member of the Cooper family. Mrs. Cooper, her son Clive, and her daughter Jill are very proud of Sheila and wash her every weekend. Sometimes they also wash her on Tuesdays. With Persil.
No wash for Sheila on this Tuesday afternoon in October. Mr. Cooper is still at the factory, and Jill is still at the office. She is a secretary. But Clive and Mrs. Cooper are at home. Mrs. Cooper is making a pie for supper, and Clive is watching television.

"Clive, come here a minute!" Mrs. Cooper calls from the kitchen, but Clive just sits and watches. "Clive!" Mrs. Cooper comes into the living-room: "You must come when I call you, Clive. What is this programme? Oh, Clive! It's a story for very young children. It's about three little pigs! And you are twelve next birthday. Have you no homework?"
"Sorry, Mummy, no, Mummy."
"Is that really true? Have you no German homework?"

"Our German teacher is ill, Mummy."

"And your English teacher?"

"We have no English homework on a Tuesday, Mummy."

"All right. Then you can go to the supermarket for me and buy a pound of tomatoes. I want to make a tomato soup for supper. Here are ten pence, and be quick!"

Clive takes the money and goes downstairs. The Coopers live on the sixth floor of a big block of flats. Outside, his friend Robin Bell is washing his father's car, a big old 1957 Jaguar.

"I don't know why you wash the poor old thing. It's so old and so slow, too slow for my grandmother!"

"You and your silly little Mini!" says Robin. "It's too small for my grandmother and much too small for my dog. By the way, where is your Mini?"

Clive looks very astonished. "Isn't Sheila standing behind your car, Robin?"

"No, she isn't. You can see that. Perhaps your father has her?"

"No, he hasn't. He never takes her to the factory. He always cycles to work, Robin."

"Yes, of course, I remember, Clive. But where is your car?"

"Let's go to the petrol station at the corner and ask Mr. Brown. Perhaps he knows where Sheila is."

"That's a very good idea, Clive. I hope nobody has stolen the car!"

"Oh, I hope not, Robin!"

Mr. Brown at the petrol station is very busy. He is selling eight gallons of Esso Extra to a fat woman in a Rolls Royce.

"Have you seen Sheila, Mr. Brown?" Clive asks him.

"No, I haven't. Don't disturb me now. I'm busy!"

"Oh dear! I must find her. Where can she be? It's awful!"

"The poor little girl!" the fat woman cries.
"Sheila is a car, Madam," Mr. Brown explains to the woman in the Rolls Royce. Then he turns to Clive and says:
"Don't worry. Probably your father is driving your Mini at this moment."
"No, he isn't, Mr. Brown. He never takes our car out on a weekday."
"Well, thank you very much, Mr. Brown," Robin says. "We must go and find that car."

Clive and Robin run back to their house. A small boy is playing ball in the front garden. He is five and very silly. "Oi, Jack! Come here a minute!" Clive calls. "Have you seen our car?"
"Your red Mini? Sheila?"
"Yes, of course!"
"A man has taken her," says the small boy and kicks the ball into the roses.
"What man? My father?"
"No, a man in a blue rain-coat, with red hair and very big feet. Yes, with enormous feet. Do you want to know his name?"
"Yes, what's his name?" Robin asks.
"I don't know," says the silly boy and runs into the house.
"Young boys today are awful!" says Robin. "What can we do?"

"You wait here for my father and tell him about Sheila. I must go to my sister's office. She has a motor scooter. Perhaps we can find the man with the red hair."
"All right, Clive. Good luck, and be careful!"

Jill and her scooter

Jill Cooper works in the office of a Nylon Stocking Factory. She is seventeen and gets £6 a week and twelve pairs of nylon stockings a year. Free! But Jill is very careful with her money. She has saved for eighteen months and bought a Vespa motor scooter. She drives it very well and looks very pretty on it. The boys in the block of flats call her the Vespa Queen of Green Lane.

Clive stands outside the factory gates and waits for Jill. She finishes work at half past five. It is twenty past five now. Ten minutes later the factory hooter goes, and the workers cycle out of the gates. Then Jill comes on her scooter. "Hallo, Clive! Why are you waiting here? Is something wrong?"
"Yes, there is! Somebody has taken our Sheila!"
"Don't be silly. Isn't she standing outside our house?"

"No, she isn't. And she isn't at the garage. A boy in our house says, a man with red hair has taken our Mini."

"Well, we must find it. Jump on, Clive!"

"Where are we going?"

"First back to Green Lane. We must ask all the neighbours. Perhaps somebody has seen our Sheila."

In Green Lane, Jill and Clive ask many people — the butcher at number four, Mr. Smith the milkman and Mrs. Black the assistant in the baker's shop. At the corner they meet Mike the paper-boy.

"How's life, Clive? You look very sad. What's wrong?" Mike asks.

"We can't find our car, Mike. Have you seen it?"

"Now wait a minute. It's a red Mini, isn't it? 235 GUY! Am I right?"

"Yes, you're quite right, Mike. How can you remember the number?"

"I can remember dozens of numbers, Clive. I'm a member of the number club."

"Yes, yes, Mike. But have you seen our car?"

"Well, yes, I have."

'When?"

"Oh, about four o'clock. A man with red hair was in it. Was it your uncle, perhaps, Clive?"

"No, Mike, not my uncle, but a thief!"

"Oh dear, I'm very sorry, Clive."

"What can we do now, Jill?" Clive asks.

"Perhaps I can help you," says Mike. "Your car was on the road to the M5 motorway. Go to the Stanton Café on the M5 ten miles from Worcester. My friend Adrian is a waiter there. And he is also secretary of the RNC."

"Good heavens! What's that?" Jill asks.

"The Registration Number Club, of course. We collect car registration numbers, long ones and funny ones, new ones and old ones. It's very interesting. I'm a member. We watch cars, talk about cars, dream about cars. Perhaps Adrian has seen the man with the red hair in your Mini."

"That's a wonderful idea!" cries Jill. "Jump on, Clive! We're going to the café on the M5!"

Fish and chips in a barn

The M5 motorway goes from Birmingham to Bristol. On this Tuesday evening in October it is full of cars and heavy lorries. It is already dark now, but Jill is a good and careful driver. She doesn't drive too fast, only thirty-five miles an hour. After fifty minutes, Jill sees the lights of the big Stanton Café. Clive parks the scooter for her. Then they go into the Help Yourself part of the café and ask for the waiter Adrian. "He's working in the big restaurant today," the woman behind the counter explains, "but he's free at seven o'clock. You can wait for him here and have a cup of tea."

"All right, thank you," Jill says. "Two cups of tea and two chocolate biscuits, please."

"That's ten pence, dear."

"I've got ten pence," Clive says. Then he remembers. Those ten pence are for the tomatoes. "Good heavens! I've just remembered," he says to his sister, "Mummy is still waiting for me and the tomatoes. And she doesn't know where we are. I hope she isn't worried."

"We can telephone her from here later," Jill answers. "Let's sit over there by the window."

At five past seven a tall boy of 17 comes into the café, and the assistant tells him about Clive and Jill. The boy comes over to their table.

"Hallo, you two. I hear you want to see me. My name is Adrian Barnes."
"Hallo, Adrian. I am Clive Cooper, and this is my sister Jill. Mike, the paper-boy from Green Lane, says you can help us."
"I'll do what I can," Adrian replies. "How is Mike?"
"Oh, he's fine. You see . . ."
Then Clive and Jill tell Adrian about their car Sheila and about the man with the red hair.
"Have you seen him or our red Mini, Adrian?" Jill asks.
"I think I know the man with red hair," Adrian answers. "He comes into our café nearly every day. We call him Jumbo."

"Why Jumbo?"

"Oh, he has enormous feet," Adrian answers.

"That's the thief of our car," Clive shouts. "Right, Jill?"

"Right, Clive!" Jill replies.

Adrian smiles and says: "Now let me think about your car. A red Mini, you say?" Adrian goes to the tea counter and talks to the assistant there. Then he comes back; he is very excited: "The assistant says Jumbo was here at half past four, and he was in a red Mini!"

"That's wonderful," cries Jill; "we're beginning to solve this crime. Now we must find out where Jumbo and our car are tonight. Have you an answer to that question, Adrian?"

"Sorry, I haven't. But perhaps our club members of the RNC can help. We're meeting tonight in Twynning."

"What's Twynning?" Clive asks.

"It's a village two miles from here. We're meeting on the farm of our president, Bob Holder. He's a very clever boy and he has a Mini, too. But it's dark blue. Can you come?"

"Give me five minutes," Jill says. "I must telephone our neighbour in Birmingham. Perhaps Mummy is worried, and we must tell her we're O. K." But

Jill comes back in two minutes. "Our neighbour isn't at home. I can't get a reply," she explains. "You can try again later," Adrian says. "Let's go to Twynning now. Follow my bike".

Ten minutes later, Jill, Clive and Adrian arrive in the middle of the old village. Adrian leads them down a narrow lane to a big farm. A dog is barking. The farm-house is dark, but a light comes from the open door of the barn. They go inside. There are perhaps twenty boys and girls sitting in the straw and drinking Coca-Cola. A tall boy with very long black hair gets up: "Hallo, Adrian! Who are your friends?" "This is our president Bob Holder," Adrian explains. "Bob, meet Jill and Clive Cooper. They live in Mike's street in Birmingham and are looking for their car."
Then Adrian tells Bob the long story.
"Come and sit down," Bob tells them. "Have a bottle of Coca-Cola. Ah, and here's Peter with our supper!"
A small, fat boy comes into the barn with an enormous parcel. Bob opens it, and inside there are twenty portions of fried fish and golden brown, hot chips.
"Get two more portions," Bob tells the boy. "And tell my mother at the Church Hall we are having

two guests tonight. Now Jill, what's the number of your car?"

Bob and the other members get out their note-books and write down the registration number of Sheila. Suddenly one boy shouts:

"I've already got that number. It's the Mini on the Cheltenham road this afternoon!"

No time to lose

In their flat in Green Lane, Birmingham, Mr. and Mrs. Cooper are having supper. But Mrs. Cooper isn't eating much.

"You must eat a little, dear!" Mr. Cooper says.

"I can't, Alan. I'm too worried. Where are our children?

What are they doing? Perhaps they're in hospital. I don't like it. It's quite dark now.

And they are out on the scooter."

"I know, dear, but Jill is seventeen and a very careful driver."

"And then your car, Alan. Perhaps the children find the thief.

What then?"

At that moment there is a knock at the front door.

Mr. Cooper opens it. A postman is standing outside and gives him a telegram.

"Oh dear, oh dear! The children are in hospital. I know it!" Mrs. Cooper cries. Mr. Cooper opens the telegram and reads it aloud:

YOUR SON CLIVE COOPER HAS PASSED HIS EXAM STOP CAN HAVE FREE PLACE AT RUGBY SCHOOL STOP MUST COME FOR INTERVIEW THURSDAY 10.00 HRS OCTOBER 12TH STOP SIGNED
DICKINSON HEADMASTER

"That's wonderful. A free place at a famous boarding school!"

"Yes, Alan," Mrs. Cooper replies, "but the interview is on Thursday, the day after tomorrow. And we don't know where Clive is. We must find him! Don't just stand there! Find him!"

"Oh, all right, dear."

Mr. Cooper puts his coat on and goes to the police station.

The policeman behind the counter is reading a letter. He is reading it very slowly.

"Excuse me," Mr. Cooper says.

"Just a moment, sir," the policeman replies.

"But this is very important. My son and my daughter are missing!"

The policeman gets up very slowly, and says: "You are Mr. Cooper, aren't you? Your red Mini is missing, isn't it? And now your children are missing, too? You're a bit careless, aren't you?"

"No, I'm not!" Mr. Cooper is angry. "Have you found my car yet?"

"No, sir, sorry, sir. It's not so easy. Sometimes we never find a stolen car," the policeman says.

"But we must find it. You see, my son and my daughter are trying to catch the thief, and that is perhaps very dangerous."

"You don't know the children of today, sir," says the policeman and smiles. It is a sour smile. "How old is your son, sir?"

"He's only twelve, but my daughter is seventeen," Mr. Cooper answers.

"Well, then you mustn't worry, sir. A girl of seventeen can look after your son. Wait until tomorrow."

"I hope you are right. My wife is very worried. I'll come back tomorrow morning, and then I'll want to see the inspector. We must find my son. He has an important interview on Thursday. There is no time to lose!"

The plan to find the thief

It is getting cold now in the barn, and the children are standing in a circle round Bob, their president. He is just saying:

"So you've seen the red Mini on the road to Cheltenham?"

"Yes, this afternoon," a boy replies.

"This is Tony," Bob explains to Clive and Jill. „He works on a farm near the Cheltenham road."

"And who was inside the Mini?" Jill asks.

"Oh, a man with red hair," Tony replies.

"Jumbo!" Adrian, Clive and Jill shout. "He's the car thief!" they explain to Bob. "He comes to the Café on the M5 nearly every day, and always in a different car."

"Right," says Bob, "now we must think hard. How can we catch Jumbo?"

"He probably has a garage in Cheltenham," says Tony.

"Yes, you're probably right," answers Bob. "We must go to Cheltenham early tomorrow morning." "Before he sells the car!" says Adrian. "Who is free tomorrow morning? You, Jack? And you, Margaret? Good. You can come with Adrian in my Mini. Jill and Clive can follow on the scooter."

"How many garages are there in Cheltenham?" Jill asks.

"Get the book, Adrian!" Bob says. "The answer is in our Royal Automobile Club book."

Adrian opens a large book and reads aloud:

Cheltenham, population 73,653. Distance to London 98 miles. 14 hotels; 11 garages.

"Does the book give the names and addresses of the garages?" Bob asks. "It does? Then copy them.

Jill and Clive can visit the first three. You, Adrian, and Margaret go to the fourth, fifth and sixth, and Jack and I can visit the rest."

"When do we meet here?" Jack asks.

"Well, you know the old proverb: 'The early bird catches the worm'. Let's meet here at seven o'clock. Right, until tomorrow morning. Good night, everybody."

Bob goes over to Clive and Jill and says: "It's nine o'clock now. You can't drive back to Birmingham tonight. Please stay with us at the farm tonight. I've already sent a boy to tell my mother. Come to the house and meet her."

Jill and Clive follow Bob into the big kitchen of the farm-house, and he tells his mother the story of Jumbo and the car called Sheila. Mrs. Holder listens and then says to Jill and Clive:

"Your beds are ready. You must be very tired. But first you must telephone your parents. Then you can have some cocoa. The telephone is in the living-room, Jill."

Jill again telephones her mother's neighbour in Birmingham, but she can't get a reply.

"She sometimes goes away for a week and visits her old mother in London," Clive says. "You must try again in the morning," Mrs. Holder replies. "Now drink this hot cocoa and go to bed."

"I'll call you at six o'clock," Bob promises. "I have an alarm clock. Sleep well!"
But Jill and Clive are too excited and lie awake for a long time.

Cheap cars for sale

"Jill, wake up!" Clive is shaking his sister.
"What's the time? Is it six o'clock already?"
"I don't know," says Clive, "but listen! What's this strange noise?" Jill sits up and listens. "It's the cows, you silly boy. We are on a farm here. Or don't you remember?"
Clive goes to the window and draws the curtains. It is still dark outside. Jill looks at her watch. "It's only half past five, Clive!" "I'm sorry, Jill," Clive says. "I can't sleep. Let's get up now." Clive goes out to the bathroom and finds Bob there.
"Heavens, you're up early!" Bob says.
"I can't sleep," Clive explains, "I'm too excited. And then the cows . . ."
"Right. Have a wash and then come downstairs to the kitchen. I'll cook a big breakfast for us." At six o'clock they are all sitting round the big table in the farm-kitchen. First they have porridge with cream and sugar, then bacon, sausages and

tomatoes. They finish with toast and marmalade and large cups of strong tea.

It is half past six now. Jill and Clive thank Mrs. Holder, and she says: "Don't mention it. You must come again and stay for a weekend. Then Bob can show you the farm — and the cows! Now be careful in Cheltenham! Call the police when you find the thief. I'll telephone your neighbour again at eight o'clock and I'll send a telegram to your father. Good luck!"
"Thank you again, Mrs. Holder," Jill replies.

Bob, Jill and Clive go out to the barn. Five minutes later, Jack, Margaret and Adrian arrive and get into Bob's Mini. Jill and Clive climb on the scooter. Bob gives them the three addresses on a piece of paper and says: "Visit these three garages in Cheltenham. Look for a man with red hair and big feet. Don't do anything. Just look and report to me. We'll meet again in front of the Cheltenham Town Hall at nine o'clock, Right?"
"Right," says Jill. Then she starts her scooter and follows Bob's Mini.

There is not much traffic on the Cheltenham road so early in the morning. The sun is shining, and the birds are singing. Clive and Jill feel happy and sing:

"Come, follow me . . ."

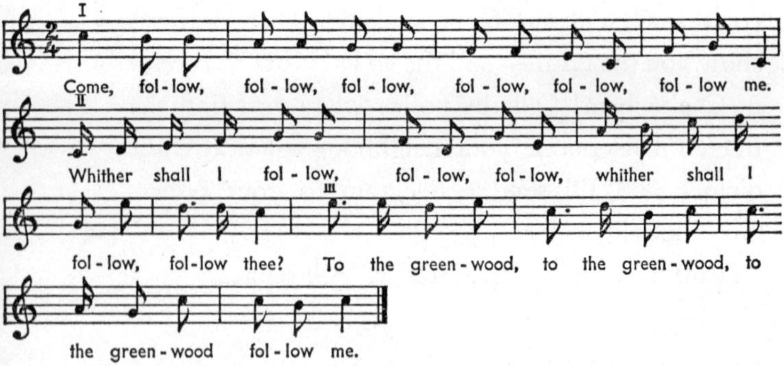

At a quarter past eight they arrive in Cheltenham. The shops are still shut, but the garages are open. Clive and Jill ask a postman for the way to the first garage on their list. It is at the other end of the town. There is a lot of traffic now. The people of Cheltenham are driving to work.

After twenty minutes, Clive and Jill find the garage, but there is only an old man inside. "Can I help you?" the old man asks. Suddenly Clive has an idea. He asks: "We're looking for a man with red hair. He probably works in a garage in Cheltenham. Do you know him?" The old man shakes his head and then says: "I'll ask my son."

His son is only eight years old, but he knows the man with red hair: "That's Gordon Benson. He has a small garage behind the Grammar School."

"Where is this Grammar School?" Jill asks.

"Go back to the corner and turn left. Then right at the next corner and left again."

"O. K., thank you very much for your help!"

Jill and Clive run back to their scooter, turn left, right, and left again, and suddenly see a big school in front of them. They park the scooter in the teacher's car park. It is still empty at this time. Then they go to a narrow road at the back of the school. Jill sees the garage first. "There it is!" she cries. Over the garage hangs a big sign: "Cheap Cars For Sale."

"Let's look inside, Jill," Clive says.

They go to the door. A man is standing in front of a dark green Mini. He has his back to them, but they can see his red hair and his enormous feet.

"It's Jumbo!" Jill says, very excited, "but I can't see our car."

"No, our car isn't here," Clive answers.

They stand for a minute and look at the six cars in the garage. Suddenly Clive cries: "Look, Jill, there is our number plate on the floor!" "Yes, and look, beside it there's a large tin of green paint!" Jill cries.

The man with the red hair hears them and turns round. Then he comes quickly to the door.

"Quick, Clive, run! He mustn't catch us!" Jill shouts.

"Hoi, you! Stop! I want to speak to you!" the man shouts.

But Jill and Clive are already round the corner and are running to their scooter.

Just in time!

At ten to nine, Jill and Clive park in front of Cheltenham Town Hall.
Bob and the others are already waiting for them.
"I'm sorry, Jill, we can't find the right garage," Bob says.
"Nobody knows this man with red hair," Adrian says.
"I can't understand it. Jumbo must work in a garage in this town," Jack says.
"You're quite right," Clive cries. He is very excited and tells them about the garage behind the Grammar School and about the tin of green paint.
"Oh, I understand," Bob says. "Our friend Jumbo has painted your red Mini green and has changed the number plates. We must go back to the garage at once before he sells your Sheila! Jack, go to the police station and tell them to come to the garage. Right? But give us fifteen minutes. We want to talk to Jumbo first. Right?"
"Right, Bob," says Jack.
"Now listen," Bob says to Jill and Clive. "You must stay outside the garage. Jumbo has already seen you and mustn't see you again.
Only come into the garage when I whistle. Right?"
"Right!" says Clive.
"What is your plan?" Jill asks Bob.

"I'll try to buy your car from Jumbo," Bob explains. "Now let's go. There's no time to lose!" They quickly drive to the garage. Jill and Clive stay outside, but Bob, Adrian and Margaret go inside.

"Good morning, sir," Jumbo says to Bob. "I'll be free in a minute." Then he turns to an old lady and her husband:

"This green Mini is a wonderful car. It's nearly new, and you can have it for £ 399."

"That's very cheap," says the husband.

"That is very, very cheap!" says Jumbo.

"But I don't like the colour," the old lady says and shakes her head. She is wearing an enormous hat with flowers and fruit salad on top.

"I want a red car. Red is my lucky colour."

"Green is also a very nice colour," says the husband, "and we need a car with a good engine. This car is nearly new. We'll buy it!"

"Stop!" Bob shouts. "You can't buy that car!"

"Why not?" asks the old lady. She is very astonished.

"That car is a stolen car, Madam," Bob explains. "It belongs to a Mr. Alan Cooper."

"Nonsense! Be quiet!" says Jumbo. He is very angry. "Get out and don't come back. I don't like jokes."

But Bob, Adrian and Margaret don't go. "This man is a thief," they explain to the old lady and her husband. Jumbo is quite red in the face now. "Ted, come here a minute," he shouts.

A very large man comes from the back of the garage. "Throw these children out!" Jumbo tells him. But Bob is not afraid.

He whistles, and Jill and Clive run into the garage.

"This is Jill Cooper," Bob tells the old lady, "and this Mini is her father's car."

"You're talking nonsense," Jumbo says. "What colour is your father's car, Miss?" he asks Jill.

"It's red," Jill replies.

"And what is its registration number?"

"It's 235 GUY," Jill answers.

"Now look at the number plate of this green Mini," Jumbo says to the old lady and her husband. "It's OFK 488 D, isn't it? You can see, these children are lying."

"No, we're not!" Jill cries. "This is our car!"

"Can you prove it?" Jumbo asks and laughs.

"Yes, I can," Jill says to the old lady. "Please open the door of this Mini and look at the left back seat. There is a big yellow spot there. My aunt's dachshund Fritzi came with us in our car last Sunday and then ..."

The old lady looks into the car and then says to Jill:

"You're quite right, dear. There is a big yellow spot there."

Jumbo turns to Ted: "That's enough. Throw these children out! Now!!"

There is a reward

"Just a moment, sir! Perhaps we can help," says a very large policeman. He is standing in the garage door. Behind him there is a police car with two policemen and Jack in it.

"That boy in the car says this green Mini is a stolen car. Please show me your papers for this car, sir!" the policeman says to Jumbo. But Jumbo doesn't answer. He and Ted run to the back door, open it . . . and there they see two other policemen, a police inspector, and Mr. Cooper, Clive's father.

"Good morning, Mr. Bloggs," says the inspector.

"Good morning, Mr. Bloggs," says Mr. Cooper

"My name isn't Bloggs. It's Benson, Gordon Benson," Jumbo says.

"We know better." The police inspector smiles. "You are Sebastian Bloggs, the Birmingham car thief. And this time you are unlucky, Bloggs!"

The inspector takes him back into the garage, and Mr. Cooper follows.

"Hallo, Dad, are you O.K.?" Clive cries.

Mr. Cooper and the police inspector laugh. "Are *you* O.K., children?"

"Of course we are. But you've come just in time. Jumbo is very angry."

"Who's Jumbo?" the police inspector and Jumbo ask.

"Jumbo is the man with the big feet," Jill explains and points to Sebastian Bloggs' feet.

"You . . . you awful child!" shouts Mr. Sebastian Bloggs.

"I'm not a child," Jill says. She is angry now.

"Don't listen to him," says the inspector. "Think of the reward!"

"What reward?" Jill and Clive ask.

"Fifty pounds," the inspector says. "Fifty pounds reward for finding this dangerous car thief. Thank you very much for your help!"

"And there is a big surprise for you, Clive," says Mr. Cooper.

"You've passed the exam, and now you have a free place at Rugby School. Isn't that wonderful?"

"It's fab!" Clive shouts.

"You have an interview tomorrow morning at ten," his father explains. Bob and Adrian congratulate Clive, and Clive says:

"Dad, meet my new friends."

Mr. Cooper smiles, thanks them and then says: "Now you must all come with me!"

"Where are we going, Dad?" Jill asks.

"To the police station, and later to the best restaurant in Cheltenham. For an enormous lunch!"

"And we are all hungry," Clive says to the others. "Right?"

"Right!" they all say and laugh.

The End

Can you answer these questions?

1 What is Mrs. Cooper making for supper on this Tuesday afternoon?
2 Where in the block of flats do the Coopers live?
3 Where can you buy petrol?
4 What is the man with red hair wearing?
5 Where does Clive wait for his sister Jill?
6 What do the members of the Number Club do?
7 Who is Bob Holder and where does he live?
8 On what are the boys in the barn sitting?
9 What is Rugby School?
10 Is Mr. Cooper as worried as Mrs. Cooper?
11 Where does Mr. Cooper go?
12 Do the police always find a stolen car?
13 Who is free to go with Bob and Clive to Cheltenham?
14 How far is Cheltenham from London?
15 Why is the neighbour of Jill's mother not at home?
16 Has Bob got a cuckoo clock?
17 When does Clive wake up the next morning?
18 Do you like porridge?
19 Do you drink strong tea for breakfast?
20 What does Mrs. Holder do at eight o'clock?
21 Is the weather bad that morning?
22 Where is Gordon Benson's garage?
23 Where does Bob meet Jill and Clive at ten to nine?
24 How much does the green Mini cost now?
25 What is the old lady wearing?
26 Who is the very large man at the back of the garage?
27 Where is the big yellow spot?
28 What is Jumbo's other name?
29 How much is the reward?
30 Where does Mr. Cooper take them for lunch?

Vocabulary — Wörterverzeichnis

café	['kæfei]	Café
M 5 (Motorway 5)	['məutəwei]	Autobahn 5

A car called Sheila

3	**car**	[kɑː]	Auto
	called	[kɔːld]	namens
	Sheila	['ʃiːlə]	weibl. Vorname
	do you like?	[duː juː laik]	magst du?
	name	[neim]	Name
	I do!		Ja, ich mag ihn!
	to know	[nəu]	kennen
	girl	[gəːl]	Mädchen
	all	[ɔːl]	alle
	nice	[nais]	nett
	but	[bʌt]	aber
	true	[truː]	wahr
	story	['stɔːri]	Geschichte
	new	[njuː]	neu
	red	[red]	rot
	Mini	['mini]	Automarke d. BLMC-Werke
	registration number	[redʒis'treiʃən]	Auto-Kennzeichen
	to belong to	[bi'lɔŋ]	gehören
	Alan Cooper	['ælən 'kuːpə]	männl. Vorname und Familienname
	Green Lane	[griːn lein]	Grüner Weg
	Birmingham	['bəːmiŋəm]	Großstadt in Mittelengland
	to love	[lʌv]	lieben
	member	['membə]	Mitglied
	family	['fæmili]	Familie
	son	[sʌn]	Sohn
	Clive	[klaiv]	männl. Vorname
	daughter	['dɔːtə]	Tochter
	Jill	[dʒil]	weibl. Vorname

very	['veri]	sehr
proud of	['praud əv]	stolz auf
to wash	[wɔʃ]	waschen
every	['evri]	jeder, jede, jedes
weekend	['wi:k'ənd]	Wochenende
sometimes	['sʌmtaimz]	manchmal
also	['ɔ:lsəu]	auch
on Tuesdays	[ɔn 'tju:zdiz]	dienstags
with	[wið]	mit
Persil	['pə:sil]	Waschpulvermarke
no wash	[wɔʃ]	keine Wagenwäsche
afternoon	['ɑ:ftə'nu:n]	Nachmittag
October	['ɔktəubə]	Oktober
still	[stil]	noch
factory	['fæktəri]	Fabrik
office	['ɔfis]	Büro
secretary	['sekrətri]	Sekretärin, Stenotypistin
at home	[ət həum]	zu Hause
to make	[meik]	machen, bereiten
pie	[pai]	Pastete, Auflauf
for supper	[fə 'sʌpə]	zum Abendbrot
to watch television	[wɔtʃ 'teliviʒən]	fernsehen
come here a minute	['minit]	komm mal eine Minute her
to call	[kɔ:l]	rufen
from	[frɔm]	aus
kitchen	['kitʃin]	Küche
just	[dʒʌst]	einfach, gerade
to sit	[sit]	sitzen
to come	[kʌm]	kommen
living-room	['liviŋrum]	Wohnzimmer
you must	[mʌst]	du mußt aber
when I call you	[kɔ:l]	wenn ich dich rufe
programme	['prəugræm]	Programm
young	[jʌŋ]	jung
children	['tʃildrən]	Kinder
It's about	[ə'baut]	es handelt von

little	['litl]	klein
pig	[pig]	Schwein
next birthday	[nekst 'bə:θdei]	an deinem nächsten Geburtstag
homework	['həumwə:k]	Hausarbeiten
sorry	['sɔri]	entschuldige bitte
Mummy	['mʌmi]	Mutti
is that really true?	['riəli tru:]	stimmt das auch wirklich?
German	['dʒə:mən]	Deutsch
4 **German teacher**	['dʒə:mən'ti:tʃə]	Deutschlehrer
ill	[il]	krank
English teacher	['iŋgliʃ'ti:tʃə]	Englischlehrer
all right	[ɔ:l 'rait]	na schön
then	[ðen]	dann
you can go	[kən gəu]	du kannst gehen
supermarket	['sju:pəma:kit]	Selbstbedienungsladen
to buy	[bai]	kaufen
pound of tomatoes	[paund əv tə'ma:təuz]	Pfund Tomaten
I want to	[wɔnt]	ich möchte
tomato soup	[tə'ma:təu su:p]	Tomatensuppe
ten pence	[ten pens]	DM 0,90
be quick!	[kwik]	schnell! beeile dich!
to take	[teik]	nehmen
money	['mʌni]	Geld
to go downstairs	[gəu daun'stɛəz]	nach unten gehen
to live	[liv]	wohnen
on the sixth floor	[flɔ:]	im 6. Stock
a block of flats	[blɔk əv 'flæts]	Wohnbl. Mietshaus
outside	['aut 'said]	draußen
friend	[frend]	Freund(in)
Robin Bell	['rɔbin bel]	männl. Vorname mit Familienname
father	['fa:ðə]	Vater
old	[əuld]	alt
Jaguar	['dʒægjuə]	br. Automarke

5 **why**	[wai]	warum
poor	[puə]	arm
thing	[θiŋ]	Ding
slow	[sləu]	langsam
too	[tuː]	zu
grandmother	[ˈgrænmʌðə]	Großmutter
silly	[ˈsili]	dumm
small	[smɔːl]	klein
much	[mʌtʃ]	viel
dog	[dɔg]	Hund
by the way	[bai ðə wei]	übrigens
where?	[wɛə]	wo?
to look	[luk]	aussehen
astonished	[əsˈtɔniʃd]	erstaunt
to stand	[stænd]	stehen
behind	[biˈhaind]	hinter
to see	[siː]	sehen
perhaps	[pəˈhæps]	vielleicht
never	[ˈnevə]	nie
always	[ˈɔːlwəz]	immer
to cycle	[ˈsaikl]	radfahren
to work	[wəːk]	zur Arbeit
of course	[əv kɔːs]	natürlich
to remember	[riˈmembə]	erinnern
let's go	[lets gəu]	gehen wir
petrol station	[ˈpetrəl ˈsteiʃən]	Tankstelle
corner	[ˈkɔːnə]	Ecke
to ask	[ɑːsk]	fragen
Mr. Brown	[ˈmistə braun]	Herr Braun
idea	[aiˈdiə]	Idee
to hope	[həup]	hoffen
nobody	[ˈnəubədi]	niemand
has stolen	[ˈstəulən]	hat gestohlen
busy	[ˈbizi]	beschäftigt
to sell	[sel]	verkaufen
8 gallons	[ˈgælənz]	1 Gallone = 3,78 Liter
Esso Extra	[ˈesəu ˈekstrə]	Benzinmarke
fat	[fæt]	dick

woman	['wumən]	Frau
Rolls Royce	['rəulz 'rɔis]	Automarke
to disturb	[dis'tə:b]	stören
now	[nau]	jetzt, nun
Oh dear!	[əu diə]	Oh je! O du liebe Zeit!
to find	[faind]	finden
awful	['ɔ:ful]	schrecklich
6 **to cry**	[krai]	ausrufen
to explain	[iks'plein]	erklären
to turn	[tə:n]	sich drehen
Madam	['mædəm]	gnädige Frau
to say	[sei]	sagen, sprechen
don't worry	[dəunt 'wʌri]	mach dir keine Sorgen
probably	['prɔbəbli]	wahrscheinlich
to drive	[draiv]	chauffieren, fahren
at the moment	['məumənt]	gerade
weekday	['wi:kdei]	Wochentag
well	[wel]	nun
thank you very much	['θæŋkju:]	vielen Dank
to run back	[rʌn bæk]	zurücklaufen
house	[haus]	Haus
boy	[bɔi]	Junge
to play ball	[plei bɔ:l]	Ball spielen
front garden	[frʌnt 'gɑ:dn]	Vordergarten
Oi, Jack!	[ɔi dʒæk]	Heda, Hans!
to kick	[kik]	stoßen
into the roses	['rəuziz]	in das Rosenbeet
what man?	[wɔt mæn]	welcher Mann?
blue	[blu:]	blau
raincoat	['reinkəut]	Regenmantel
hair	[hɛə]	Haar
feet	[fi:t]	Füße
enormous	[i'nɔ:məs]	riesig
what's his name?	[neim]	wie heißt er?

	today	[tə'dei]	heute
	what can we do?	[du:]	was können wir nur tun?
7	**to wait**	[weit]	warten
	to tell about	[tel 'əbaut]	erzählen von
	motor-scooter	['məutə 'sku:tə]	Motorroller
	good luck!	[lʌk]	viel Glück!

Jill and her scooter

7	**to work**	[wə:k]	arbeiten
	nylon stocking	['nailən 'stɔkiŋ]	Nylonstrumpf
	to get	[get]	bekommen
	£ 6 a week	[wi:k]	DM 54 in der Woche
	twelve pairs a year	[pεəz ə jiə]	12 Paar im Jahr
	free	[fri:]	unentgeltlich
	to save	[seiv]	sparen
	month	[mʌnθ]	Monat
	very well	['veri wel]	sehr gut
	pretty	['priti]	hübsch
	Vespa Queen	['vespə kwi:n]	Motorroller
	factory gates	['fæktəri geits]	Fabriktor
	to finish	['finiʃ]	beenden
	half past five	[hɑ: pəs faiv]	17.30 Uhr
	twenty past five	['twenti]	zwanzig Minuten nach 5
	minute	['minit]	Minute
	later	['leitə]	später
	hooter	['hu:tə]	Sirene
	to start	[stɑ:t]	beginnen
	is something wrong?	['sʌmθiŋ rɔŋ]	ist etwas nicht in Ordnung
	somebody	['sʌmbədi]	irgend jemand
	garage	['gærɑ:ʒ]	Garage, Werkstatt
	jump on	['dʒʌmp'ɔn]	schwing dich rauf!
	first	[fə:st]	zuerst
	back	[bæk]	zurück

	neighbour	['neibə]	Nachbar
	many people	['meni 'piːpl]	viele Leute
	butcher	['butʃə]	Schlachter
	Mr. Smith	[smiθ]	Herr Schmidt
	milkman	['milkmən]	Milchmann
	Mrs. Black	['misiz blæk]	Frau Schwarz
	assistant	[ə'sistənt]	Verkäuferin
	baker's shop	['beikəz ʃɔp]	Bäckerladen
	to meet	[miːt]	treffen
	Mike	[maik]	Michael
	paperboy	['peipə bɔi]	Zeitungsausträger
	how is life?	[hauz laif]	wie steht's?
	sad	[sæd]	traurig
	am I right?	[rait]	hab ich recht?
	you're quite right	[kwait rait]	du hast ganz recht
	dozens of numbers	['dʌznz]	Dutzende von Nummern
	number-club	['nʌmbə klʌb]	Nummernklub
	when?	[wen]	wann?
	uncle	['ʌŋkl]	Onkel
	thief	[θiːf]	Dieb
9	**to help**	[help]	helfen
	road	[rəud]	Straße
	Stanton Café	['stæntən 'kæfei]	Autobahn Raststätte an der M 5
	mile	[mail]	1 Meile = 1609 Meter
	Worcester	['wustə]	Stadt in Mittelengland
	Adrian	['eidriən]	männlicher Vorname
	waiter	['weitə]	Kellner
	there	[ðɛə]	da, dort
	RNC		Klub der Autokennzeichen-Sammler
	good heavens!	[gud 'hevnz]	du lieber Himmel!
	what's that?	[wɔts ðæt]	was ist denn das?
	to collect	[kə'lekt]	sammeln
	long ones	[lɔŋ wʌnz]	lange

	funny	['fʌni]	komisch
	to watch	[wɔtʃ]	beobachten
	to talk about	[tɔ:k]	sprechen über
	to dream about	[dri:m]	träumen von
	wonderful	['wʌndəful]	wunderbar, großartig

Fish and chips in a barn

10	fish and chips	[fiʃ ən tʃips]	Fisch mit Pommes Frites
	barn	[ba:n]	Scheune
	Bristol	['bristl]	Hafenstadt in Westengland
	evening	['i:vniŋ]	Abend
	full of	[ful əv]	voller
	heavy	['hevi]	schwer
	lorry	['lɔri]	Lastwagen
	already	[ɔ:l'redi]	schon
	dark	[da:k]	dunkel
	driver	['draivə]	Fahrer
	fast	[fa:st]	schnell
	only	['əunli]	nur
	an hour	['auə]	in der Stunde
	after	['a:ftə]	nach
	light	[lait]	Licht
	to park	[pa:k]	parken
	Help Yourself part	[help jə'self pa:t]	Selbstbedienungsteil
	to ask for	[a:sk]	fragen nach
	restaurant	['restərɔ:ŋ]	Restaurant
	today	[tə 'dei]	heute
	behind	[bi'haind]	hinter
	counter	['kauntə]	Büfett
	free	[fri:]	frei
	to have a cup of tea	[kʌp əv ti:]	eine Tasse Tee trinken
	chocolate biscuit	['tʃɔkəlit 'biskit]	Schokoladenkeks
	please	[pli:z]	bitte
	that's ten pence	[ðæts ten pens]	das macht 10 Pence

	dear	[diə]	meine Liebe
	I've got	[aiv gɔt]	ich habe
	worried	[ˈwʌrid]	in Sorge
	to telephone	[ˈtelifəun]	anrufen
	later	[ˈleitə]	später
	to answer	[ˈɑːnsə]	antworten
	let's sit	[lets sit]	setzen wir uns
	over there	[ˈəuvə ðɛə]	dort drüben
	by the window	[bai ðə ˈwindəu]	ans Fenster
	tall	[tɔːl]	groß
	of seventeen	[əv ˈsevnˈtiːn]	17jährig
	to come over	[kʌm ˈəuvə]	herüberkommen
	table	[ˈteibl]	Tisch
11	**to hear**	[hiə]	hören
	Barnes	[bɑːnz]	Nachname
	I'll do what I can	[kæn]	ich will sehen, was sich machen läßt
	to reply	[riˈplai]	erwidern
	how is ?	[hauz]	wie geht's ?
	he's fine	[hiːz fain]	ihm geht's gut
	you see	[siː]	du mußt verstehen
	to think	[θiŋk]	glauben, denken
	nearly, almost	[ˈniəli]	fast
	every day	[ˈevri dei]	täglich, jeden Tag
12	**to shout**	[ʃaut]	ausrufen, schreien
	right ?	[rait]	habe ich recht ?
	to smile	[smail]	lächeln
	to let	[let]	lassen
	to think about	[θiŋk əˈbaut]	nachdenken über
	tea counter	[tiː ˈkauntə]	Tee Büfett
	excited	[ikˈsaitid]	aufgeregt
	to begin	[biˈgin]	anfangen
	to solve, to commit	[sɔlv]	lösen, begehen
	crime	[kraim]	Verbrechen

to find out	[faind aut]	herausfinden
tonight	[tə'nait]	heute abend
question	['kwestʃən]	Frage
Twynning	['twiniŋ]	Dorfname
village	['vilidʒ]	Dorf
farm	[fɑːm]	Bauernhof
president	['prezidənt]	Vorsitzender
Bob Holder	[bɔb 'həuldə]	Name
clever	['klevə]	klug
dark blue	[dɑːk bluː]	dunkelblau
we're O. K.	[wiə 'əu'kei]	wir sind gut aufgehoben

13	**reply**	[ri'plai]	Antwort
	to try again	[trai ə'gen]	noch einmal versuchen
	to follow	['fɔləu]	folgen
	to arrive	[ə'raiv]	ankommen
	in the middle of	['midl əv]	mitten in
	to lead	[liːd]	führen
	down a narrow lane	[daun ə 'nærəu lein]	einen schmalen Weg entlang
	to bark	[bɑːk]	bellen
	open	['əupən]	offen
	door	[dɔː]	Tür
	to go inside	[in'said]	hineingehen
	straw	[strɔː]	Stroh
	to drink	[driŋk]	trinken
	black	[blæk]	schwarz
	to get up	[get ʌp]	aufstehen
	Bob, meet Jill	[bɔb miːt dʒil]	Darf ich dir Jill vorstellen, Bob?
	street	[striːt]	Straße
	to look for	[luk fɔː]	suchen nach
	to sit down	[sit daun]	sich hinsetzen
	have a bottle	['bɔtl]	nehmt euch eine Flasche
	Peter	['piːtə]	männl. Vorname

	parcel	['pɑːsl]	Paket
	to open	['əupən]	öffnen
	inside	[in'said]	darin
	portion	['pɔːʃən]	Portion
	fried fish	[fraid fiʃ]	gebratener Fisch
	golden brown	['gəuldən braun]	goldbraun
	hot	[hɔt]	heiß
	two more	[tuː mɔː]	noch zwei
	Church Hall	[tʃəːtʃ hɔːl]	Gemeinschaftssaal d. kirchl. Gemeinde
14	guest	[gest]	Gast
	the other members	['ʌðə]	die anderen Mitglieder
	note-book	['nəutbuk]	Notizbuch
	to write down	[rait daun]	aufschreiben
	suddenly	['sʌdnli]	plötzlich
	Cheltenham	['tʃeltnəm]	Stadt in Westengland
	this afternoon	[ðis 'ɑːftə'nuːn]	heute nachmittag

No time to lose

14	no time to lose	[nəu taim tə luːz]	keine Zeit zu verlieren
	to eat	[iːt]	essen
	much	[mʌtʃ]	viel
	a little	[ə'litl]	ein wenig
	hospital	['hɔspitl]	Krankenhaus
	to like	[laik]	mögen
	quite	[kwait]	ganz
	they are out	[aut]	sind unterwegs
	there's a knock	[nɔk]	jemand klopft
	front door	[frʌnt dɔː]	Wohnungstür
15	postman	['pəustmən]	Postbote
	to give	[giv]	geben, überreichen
	telegram	['teligræm]	Telegramm
	to read aloud	[riːd ə'laud]	vorlesen
	to pass an exam	[pɑːs ən ig'zæm]	eine Prüfung bestehen

	free place	[fri: pleis]	Freiplatz, Stipendium
	Rugby School	['rʌgbi sku:l]	Public School, private Internatsschule
	interview	['intəvju:]	Interview
	Thursday	['θə:zdi]	Donnerstag
	signed	[saind]	unterschrieben
	Dickinson	['dikinsən]	Familienname
	headmaster	['hed'mɑ:stə]	Direktor
	famous	['feiməs]	berühmt
	boarding school	['bɔ:diŋ sku:l]	Internatsschule
	day after tomorrow	[dei 'ɑ:ftə tə'mɔrəu]	übermorgen
	don't just stand there	[dəunt dʒʌst stænd ðɛə]	steh nicht nur so rum!
	to put on	[put ɔn]	anziehen
	coat	[kəut]	Mantel
	police station	[pə'li:s 'steiʃən]	Polizeiwache
	policeman	[pə'li:smən]	Polizist
	letter	['letə]	Brief
	excuse me	[iks'kju:z mi]	entschuldigen Sie!
	just a moment	[dʒʌst ə 'məumənt]	nur noch einen Augenblick
	sir	[sə:]	mein Herr
16	**important**	[im'pɔ:tənt]	wichtig
	to be missing	['misiŋ]	vermißt sein
	a bit	[bit]	ein wenig
	careless	['kɛəlis]	unvorsichtig
	angry	['æŋgri]	böse
	easy	['i:zi]	leicht
	to catch	[kætʃ]	fangen
	dangerous	['deindʒrəs]	gefährlich
	to look after	[luk'ɑ:ftə]	aufpassen auf
	until	[ən'til]	bis
	tomorrow morning	[tə'mɔrəu 'mɔ:niŋ]	morgen früh
	wife	[waif]	Ehefrau
	inspector	[in'spektə]	Kriminalrat

The plan to find the thief

17	**plan**	[plæn]	Plan
	to get cold	[get kəuld]	kalt werden
	circle	['səːkl]	Kreis
	round	[raund]	herum
	Tony	['təuni]	männl. Vorname
	near	[niə]	in der Nähe von
18	**different**	['difrənt]	verschieden, anders
	to think hard	[θiŋk hɑːd]	angestrengt überlegen
	before	[bi'fɔː]	ehe
	Margaret	['mɑːgərit]	weibl. Vorname
	to follow	['fɔləu]	folgen
	how many?	[hau 'meni]	wie viele?
	Royal Automobile Club	['rɔiəl]	Königlicher Automobil Klub
	large	[lɑːdʒ]	groß
	population	[pɔpju'leiʃən]	Einwohnerzahl
	distance	['distəns]	Entfernung
	London	['lʌndən]	Br. Hauptstadt
	to give	[giv]	angeben
	address	[ə'dres]	Adresse
	to copy	['kɔpi]	abschreiben
19	**to visit**	['vizit]	aufsuchen
	the first three	[fəːst θriː]	die ersten drei
	the rest	[rest]	die restlichen
	proverb	['prɔvəːb]	Sprichwort
	the early bird catches the worm	['əːli bəːd 'kætʃiz ðə wəːm]	Wer zuerst kommt, mahlt zuerst
	good night everybody	['evribɔdi]	Gute Nacht allerseits
	to stay with	[stei wið]	bleiben bei
	to listen	['lisn]	zuhören
	bed	[bed]	Bett
	ready	['redi]	fertig, bereit
	tired	['taiəd]	müde

	parents	['pɛərənts]	Eltern
	cocoa	['kəukəu]	Kakao
	away	[ə'wei]	fort, weg
20	**to call**	[kɔːl]	rufen
	to promise	['prɔmis]	versprechen
	alarm clock	[ə'lɑːm klɔk]	Wecker
	sleep well!	[sliːp wel]	schlaft gut!
	to lie awake	[ə'weik]	wach liegen
	for a long time	[lɔŋ taim]	eine lange Zeit

Cheap cars for sale

20	**cheap cars for sale**	[tʃiːp kɑːz fə seil]	preiswerte Autos zu verkaufen
	to wake up	[weik ʌp]	aufwachen
	to shake	[ʃeik]	rütteln
	what's the time?	[wɔts ðə taim]	wie spät ist es?
	strange	[streindʒ]	eigenartig
	noise	[nɔiz]	Geräusch
	to sit up	[sit ʌp]	sich aufsetzen
	cow	[kau]	Kuh
	to draw the curtains	[drɔː ðə 'kəːtnz]	Gardinen aufziehen
	watch	[wɔtʃ]	Armbanduhr
	to get up	[get ʌp]	aufstehen
	bathroom	['bɑːθrum]	Badezimmer
	you are up early	['əːli]	du bist aber früh auf!
	have a wash	[wɔʃ]	wasch dich!
	to cook	[kuk]	kochen
	breakfast	['brekfəst]	Frühstück
	porridge	['pɔridʒ]	Haferflockenbrei
	cream	[kriːm]	Sahne
	sugar	['ʃugə]	Zucker
	bacon	['beikən]	Schinkenspeck
	sausage	['sɔsidʒ]	Bratwurst
21	**marmalade**	['mɑːməleid]	Apfelsinenmarmelade
	strong	[strɔŋ]	stark

	to thank	[θæŋk]	sich bedanken
	don't mention it	[ˈmenʃən]	gern geschehen, nicht der Rede wert
	to mention	[ˈmenʃən]	erwähnen
	again	[əˈgen]	wieder
	to show	[ʃəu]	zeigen
	police	[pəˈliːs]	Polizei
	when	[wen]	wenn
	to arrive	[əˈraiv]	ankommen
	to climb on	[klaim]	klettern auf
	piece of paper	[piːs əv ˈpeipə]	Stück Papier
	don't do anything	[ˈeniθiŋ]	nichts unternehmen
	report to me	[riˈpɔːt]	erstattet mir Bericht
	in front of	[frʌnt əv]	vor
	Town Hall	[taun hɔːl]	Rathaus
	to start	[stɑːt]	starten
	traffic	[ˈtræfik]	Verkehr
	sun	[sʌn]	Sonne
	to shine	[ʃain]	scheinen
22	**bird**	[bəːd]	Vogel
	to sing	[siŋ]	singen
	to feel happy	[fiːl ˈhæpi]	sich glücklich fühlen
	a quarter past	[ˈkwɔːtə pɑːst]	Viertel nach
	shut	[ʃʌt]	geschlossen
	to ask the way	[ɑːsk ðə wei]	den Weg erfragen
	first	[fəːst]	erste
	list	[list]	Liste
	end	[end]	Ende
	town	[taun]	Stadt
	a lot	[ə lɔt]	viel
	head	[hed]	Kopf
23	**Gordon Benson**	[ˈgɔːdənˈbensən]	Name
	Grammar School	[ˈgræmə skuːl]	Gymnasium
	to turn left	[təːn left]	links einbiegen
	right	[rait]	rechts
	school	[skuːl]	Schule
	in front of them	[frʌnt]	vor ihnen

	teachers' car park	['ti:tʃəz kɑ: pɑ:k]	Parkplatz für Lehrer
	empty	['empti]	leer
	at this time	[æt ðis taim]	zu dieser Zeit
	There it is!	['ðɛəritiz]	Da ist sie!
	over	['əuvə]	über
	to hang	[hæŋ]	hängen
	sign	[sain]	Schild
	back	[bæk]	Rücken
	floor	[flɔ:]	Fußboden
	beside	[bi'said]	daneben
	tin	[tin]	Dose
	paint	[peint]	Ölfarbe
24	**quick**	[kwik]	schnell
	to speak	[spi:k]	sprechen

Just in time!

25	**Just in time!**	[dʒʌst in taim]	Gerade zur rechten Zeit!
	right	[rait]	richtig
	to understand	[ʌndə'stænd]	verstehen
	to paint	[peint]	malen
	to change	[tʃeindʒ]	wechseln, ändern
	number plate	['nʌmbə pleit]	Nummernschild
	at once	[ət wʌns]	sofort
	to whistle	['wisl]	pfeifen
26	**lady**	['leidi]	Dame
	husband	['hʌzbənd]	Ehemann
	colour	['kʌlə]	Farbe
	to wear	[wɛə]	tragen
	hat	[hæt]	Hut
	flower	['flauə]	Blume
	fruit salad	[fru:t'sæləd]	Obstsalat
	on top	[ɔn tɔp]	oben drauf
	lucky	['lʌki]	glückbringend
	to need	[ni:d]	brauchen

	engine	['endʒin]	Motor
	nonsense!	['nɔnsəns]	Unsinn!
	joke	[dʒəuk]	Witz
27	**red in the face**	[feis]	vor Zorn rot im Gesicht
	Ted	[ted]	Eduard
	back	[bæk]	der hintere Teil
	to throw out	[θrəu 'aut]	hinauswerfen
	to be afraid	[ə'freid]	Angst haben
	Miss	[mis]	Fräulein
	to lie	[lai]	lügen
	to prove	[pruːv]	beweisen
	to laugh	[lɑːf]	lachen
	back seat	[bæk siːt]	Rücksitz
	yellow	['jeləu]	gelb
	spot	[spɔt]	Fleck
	aunt	[ɑːnt]	Tante
	Sunday	['sʌndi]	Sonntag
28	**enough**	[i'nʌf]	genug

There is a reward

29	**reward**	[ri'wɔːd]	Belohnung
	papers	['peipəz]	Papiere
	Bloggs	[blɔgz]	Familienname
	to know better	[nəu 'betə]	es besser wissen
	Sebastian	[si'bæstiən]	männl. Vorname
	to be unlucky	[ʌn'lʌki]	Pech haben
	Dad	[dæd]	Vati
	to point to	[pɔint]	auf etwas zeigen
30	**surprise**	[sə'praiz]	Überraschung
	fab!	[fæb]	prima, fabelhaft!
	to congratulate	[kən'grætjuleit]	gratulieren
	best	[best]	bestes
	lunch	[lʌntʃ]	Mittagessen
	hungry	['hʌŋgri]	hungrig